VASILISA THE FAIR

Based on *The Frog Princess and Other Russian Folk Tales* by
Sophia Prokofieva & Irina Tokmakova

Music by
Alla Lander

Translated by
Sabina Modzhalevskaya & Harlow Robinson

Adapted by
Adrian Mitchell

Originally commissioned and produced by
New York State Theatre Institute

SAMUEL FRENCH, INC.

Also Available from Samuel French

MORE WONDERFUL PLAYS AND MUSICALS
THAT WERE ORIGINALLY PRODUCED BY
THE NEW YORK THEATRE INSTITUTE

The Canterville Ghost

The Killings Tale

A Little Princess

Miracle on 34th Street

Sherlock's Secret Life

The Snow Queen

A Tale of Cinderella

VASILISA
THE FAIR

Based on *The Frog Princess and Other Russian Folk Tales* by
Sophia Prokofieva & Irina Tokmakova

Music by
Alla Lander

Translated by
Sabina Modzhalevskaya & Harlow Robinson

Adapted by
Adrian Mitchell

Originally commissioned and produced by
New York State Theatre Institute

SAMUEL FRENCH, INC.

45 West 25th Street   7623 Sunset Boulevard
NEW YORK 10010   HOLLYWOOD 90046
LONDON   TORONTO

IMPORTANT BILLING AND CREDIT REQUIREMENTS

All producers of VASILISA THE FAIR *must* give credit to the Authors of the Play and the Producers of the initial production in all programs distributed in connection with performances of the Play and in all instances in which the title of the Play appears for purposes of advertising, publicizing or otherwise exploiting the Play and/or a production. The name of the Authors *must* also appear on a separate line, on which no other name appears, immediately following the title, and *must* appear in size of type not less than fifty percent the size of the title type. The name of the Producer of the initial production *must* appear on a separate line in which no other matter appears, immediately following the Author, and must be in size of type not less than 50% of the size type used for the Author. Credits should be substantially as follows:

VASILISA THE FAIR

Based on *The Frog Princess and Other Russian Folk Tales* by
Sophia Prokofieva and Irina Tokmakova

Music by
Alla Lander

Translated by
Sabina Modzhalevskaya and Harlow Robinson

Adapted by
Adrian Mitchell

Originally commissioned and produced by
New York State Theatre Institute

New York State Theatre Institute
Patricia Di Benedetto Snyder, Producing Artistic Director
presents

VASILISA
THE FAIR

Based on *The Frog Princess and Other Russian Folk Tales* by
Sophia Prokofieva and Irina Tokmakova

Music by
Alla Lander

Translated by
Sabina Modzhalevskaya and Harlow Robinson

Adapted by
Adrian Mitchell

Set Design by Richard Finkelstein
Costume Design by Brent Griffin
Lighting Design by John McLain
Sound Design by Matt Elie
Orchestrator / Arranger Vladimir Polezhayev
Musical Supervisor Betsy Riley-Normile
Production Stage Manager Robin Horowitz
Literary Manager James Farrell
Musical Director / Additional Arrangements Mark Brockley
Choreographer Raymond C. Harris

Directed by
Patrician Di Benedetto Snyder and Adrienne Posner

<u>Premiere Performance: May 11, 1991</u>

ORIGINAL CAST

The Tsar of Russia	*John Romeo*
Ivan-Tsarevich	*Richard Barrows*
Foma-Tsarevich	*David Bunce*
Danila-Tsarevich	*Michael P. Fitzgerald*
Akulina	*Betsy Riley-Normile*
Pava	*Etta Caren Fink*
Vasilisa the Fair	*Marlene Goudreau*
Kashchey the Deathless	*John Thomas McGuire III*
Misha-Medved	*Joel Aroeste*
Baba Yaga	*Joseph Larrabee-Quandt*
Stroganov-Sabaka	*David Bunce*
Golubtsy-Koshka	*Etta Caren Fink*
Zamok	*John Robert McEnerney*
Baba Yaga's Hut	*Raymond C. Harris*
Iva	*Ewa Lewinska*
Sasha-Shpionka	*Jeneane Schmidt*
The Sea Tsar	*John Romeo*
The Ensemble	*David Bunce, Etta Caren Fink, Michael P. Fitzgerald, Raymond C. Harris, Bonnie Jeanne Howland, Ewa Lewinska, Gary D. Marshall, John Robert McEnerney, Christina Patrick, Tara Raucci, Jeneane Schmidt, Jennifer Williams, Michael John Ziccardo*

Musicians

Conductor / Keyboard	*Mark Brockley*
Balalaika	*Sam Farkas*
Accordion	*Al Colesessano*
Percussion	*George Fortune*

CHARACTERS

The Tsar of Russia	
Ivan-Tsarevich	
Foma-Tsarevich	Sons of the Tsar
Danila-Tsarevich	
Akulina	Daughter of an archduke
Pava	Daughter of a silk merchant
Vasilisa the Fair	The Frog Princess, Kashchey's daughter
Kashchey the Deathless	A wicked wizard
Baba Yaga	A horrible witch
Stroganov-Sabaka	Baba Yaga's dog
Golubtsy-Koshka	Baba Yaga's cat
Zamok	Baba Yaga's gate
Iva	Baba Yaga's tree
Misha-Medved	The fire-breathing bear
Sasha-Shpionka	Serving woman Kashchey
Guard	Guard to Kashchey
The Sea Tsar	Tsar of All the Seas and Oceans
The Ensemble	Guards, evil spirits, fence, etc.

SETTINGS

ACT I

Scene 1 The Tsar's Palace   Scene 3 The Tsar's Palace
Scene 2 The Swamp   Scene 4 The Forest

ACT II

Scene 1 Baba Yaga's Hut   Scene 3 The Tsar's Palace
Scene 2 Kashchey's Palace

A NOTE ABOUT THE MUSIC

The music created by Alla Lander for *VASILISA THE FAIR* has deep roots in Russian folklore The dance music and underscoring is intended for synthesizer, balalaika, and small percussion instruments. Should you desire to create your own Russian-style music, be our guest.

A working tape of the original production for your research is available from The New York State Theatre Institute, 37 First Street, Troy , NY 12180, Attn: Patricia D. Benedetto Snyder.

ACT I

Scene 1
The Tsar's Palace

(The ENSEMBLE, the two brothers, DANILA-TSAREVICH and FOMA-TSAREVICH, and SASHA-SHPIONKA, dressed as an ensemble member, enter into the theatre from various places, cued by the overture. They assemble on the stage and commence a folk dance to the brother's flute and balalaika music. At the end of the dance a playful scuffle breaks out between the two brothers. Both laugh so hard that they fall down. They're still lying there when the TSAR, yawning and stretching, emerges on the scene.)

TSAR. What a delightful little Russian morning! Time for the Tsar to start ruling his Tsardom. Better dash off a new law and stamp it with my galumptious Imperial seal.

(FOMA-TSAREVICH and DANILA-TSAREVICH jump to their feet as if scalded.)

FOMA-TSAREVICH. Can't it wait till after breakfast.
DANILA-TSAREVICH. Please father, no more new laws.
FOMA-TSAREVICH. You've made so many already.
DANILA-TSAREVICH. All of them scribbled on scrolls.
FOMA-TSAREVICH. They're lying all over the palace—
DANILA-TSAREVICH. Laws on the stove—
FORMA-TSAREVICH. Laws on the tables—
DANILA-TSAREVICH. Laws on the chairs—
FOMA-TSAREVICH. And laws in the bath.
DANILA-TSAREVICH. There's no room to walk—
FOMA-TSAREVICH. We all trip over them.

DANILA-TSAREVICH. If you pass a law forbidding skating on Monday—

FOMA-TSAREVICH. You pass a law saying everybody has to skate on Tuesday.

DANILA-TSAREVICH. Confusion!

FOMA-TSAREVICH. Chaos!

TSAR. But I enjoy it. Writing nice new laws and sealing them up with my right royal seal. All that scarlet sealing wax spluttering and dripping and blobbing onto the parchment. And then I go plonk! With my golden seal. It's a grandillowy feeling. How could you rob me of that? But where's your brother—Ivan-Tsarevich?

FOMA-TSAREVICH. Wherever crazy people go. Did you hear what Ivan-Tsarevich did yesterday? He went out to cut the hay. Cut down a silver birch tree by mistake!

DANILA-TSAREVICH. That's nothing! Last night he went out to saddle his pony. Saddled up a wild bull! It was a great ride.

TSAR. How can the son of a Tsar waste his royal time on such idioticious dumbumfoolery? Why can't the three of you behave like ordinary children? Like I do?

(IVAN-TSAREVICH dances on. A wreath of wild flowers perches at an angle on his head. His simple embroidered Russian blouse is torn. His trousers are also the worse for wear.)

IVAN-TSAREVICH. Dear father, I wish you a glorious old age. But you don't look yourself.

TSAR. Who do I look, then?

IVAN-TSAREVICH. You look pale and drawn. Not very well. Are you suffering from a touch of the ruminogles?

TSAR. Don't worry about me—I am not the problem. I'm just a Tsar, a Tsar like any other, highly respected by my fellow Tsars. From dawn to dusk I turn out law after law like a stack of pancakes. And it's high time that you little Princes grew up and helped me handle the great frying pan in which the laws are made and tossed and caught.   DANILA-TSAREVICH. Us?

FOMA-TSAREVICH. You mean us?

DANILA-TSAREVICH. What have we done wrong?

IVAN-TSAREVICH. We didn't steal any pancakes.

TSAR. SILENCE! When the Tsar is speaking, and efferlicious silence should fall. That's better.... Listen and hark with all six of your waxy ears. I have been thinking with my brain. And while I thought I gobbled up three puff pastry pies full of succulent salmon and munchy mushrooms and I washed them down with three steaming samovars of tongue-scorching tea. And here *(Producing a scroll.)* is the result of all that eating and thinking. My dear Princes, place your hands on your hearts and make a royal vow that you'll obey this law.

FOMA-TSAREVICH. I vow, dear Father.

DANILA-TSAREVICH. I vow, dear Tsar.

FOMA-TSAREVICH and DANILA-TSAREVICH. Cross our hearts and hope to die.

IVAN-TSAREVICH. If you need my vow, you can have it any time. But I hope this scroll doesn't ask the impossible.

TSAR. Bring the Great Bow of Babylon.

(A SERVANT brings on a great bow.)

IVAN-TSAREVICH. Are you planning some kind of hunt?

TSAR. Yes indeed, a hunt, but a very special King of the Hunts. A Bride Hunt.

IVAN-TSAREVICH. What's a Bride Hunt?

TSAR. Each of you, my three plumbidious Princes, will shoot an arrow. Wherever it falls, that's where you'll find your wife.

FOMA-TSAREVICH. A wife.

DANILA-TSAREVICH. A bride?

FOMA-TSAREVICH. What do we need a wife for?

DANILA-TSAREVICH. You mean you want us to get married?

FOMA-TSAREVICH. That doesn't sound too terrible—

DANILA-TSAREVICH. In fact it sounds just great—

IVAN-TSAREVICH. Me? Get married? To a bride? Me?? And lose all my lovely freedom? Me??? Not for all the bobolinks in Bulgaria!

TSAR. And what about your royal vow? This scroll contains my new Princes Must Go on a Bride Hunt Law. Foma-Tsarevich, you first.

FOMA-TSAREVICH. See that sparkling soaring tower? That gold dome shining so fiercely that it stings your eyes? That's where my arrow longs to go. Fly strongly, fly high!

(FOMA-TSAREVICH shoots. The arrow whizzes through the air. FOMA-TSAREVICH passes the great bow to DANILA-TSAREVICH.)

TSAR. Danila-Tsarevich.

DANILA-TSAREVICH. *(Taking aim.)* You see that palace, bright and white as a gigantic sugar lump? That's where my arrow's going, with any luck. Fly sweetly, fly far!

(DANILA-TSAREVICH shoots. The whizzing of an arrow.)

TSAR. And so your turn comes round, Ivan-Tsarevich.

IVAN-TSAREVICH. *(Delaying.)* Just a minute, Father. I really ought to discuss this with my horse, you know … the black one—

TSAR. Don't talk such goggle-moggle! Shoot your arrow!

(AKULINA, an archduke's daughter, enters holding one of the golden arrows. Bowing low, she presents in to FOMA-TSAREVICH. She is very richly dressed. She has dark eyebrows and a long, dark braid.)

TSAR. Very apploobious indeed. And whose daughter are you, my dumpling?

AKULINA. I am Akulina, the Archduke's daughter. Isn't that obvious, dearest and most prehistoric Tsar of all the Russias?

(PAVA, a merchant's daughter, runs in. Bowing low, she hands the second golden arrow to DANILA-TSAREVICH. She is fair with a rosy complexion and overdressed in very bright clothes.)

TSAR. And who are you?

PAVA. Hold your hogbucklets. I'll tell you when I've finished chewing this muffin.

TSAR. I can see you're not a nun.

PAVA. *(Gulps loudly.)* My name is Pava. I'm the daughter of a seller of silken suits and satin shirts.

TSAR. You are both little beauties. *(Turns to IVAN-TSAREVICH.)* So why are you standing there like a waxwork that won't work? Shoot an arrow—win a bride. Do you follow me?

IVAN-TSAREVICH. Father—I've got a great idea. I'll nip off on a quest for the famous Firebird and I'll pluck you one of his tail feathers and carve it into a quill pen of flame which you can use to write a billion new laws—

TSAR. You heard what I— *(Corrects himself.)* You heard what the Tsar ordered—win a bride. Then you marry her. She marries you. You get married. To each other. Is that clear? Ivan-Tsarevich, shoot your arrow!

IVAN-TSAREVICH. All right, you're the Tsar. I'll shoot. Why not? Here goes.

(IVAN-TSAREVICH aims away from the city.)

TSAR. *(With a start.)* What are you aiming at, lumphead? Nobody lives in that direction. Nobody travels that way—not even hens and horses. It's all bog over there, an enormous swamp like goopy soup.

FOMA-TSAREVICH. What's wrong with you, brother?

DANILA-TSAREVICH. Nothing over there but miles of mud.

AKULINA. It's extremely malodorous.

PAVA. And it smells bad, too.

AKULINA. I wouldn't go in the swamps, not even for cloudberries—

PAVA. Not even for tadpoles.

(All try to grab IVAN-TSAREVICH and turn him toward the city.)

ALL. *(In chorus.)* That way, that way, aim over that way!

TSAR. I'm warning you, Ivan. You're deciding your future—the future of our family—the future of Russia!

IVAN-TSAREVICH. Golden arrow, fly to the empty swamp. Let marriage sink in the quagmire.

(IVAN-TSAREVICH breaks free and, without even aiming, shoots toward the swamp. The whizzing of an arrow gradually fades

away.)

TSAR. Groveling grandfathers! What a blubberbrain!

IVAN-TSAREVICH. You told me—shoot. So I shot.

TSAR. I might as well talk to my feet. All right. Now listen and hark with all ten of your tingling ears. Tomorrow I will throw a right royal banquet in my royal palace. Each of the new royal brides will bake me a royal loaf of fancy bread and embroider me a glorious tablecloth decorated with royal roosters. That I shall take a royal look at the loaves and tablecloths and judge which of the royal brides is most devoted to her royal Tsar.

AKULINA. Dear Tsar and Father, you'll fall in love with my loaf. There'll be so much sugar in it that it'll choke you.

PAVA. Dear Father and Tsar, you'll fall in love with my tablecloth. The roosters will be so life-like that they'll peck your eyes out.

TSAR. Excellent. But what about you, Ivan-Tsarevich? What happened to the third arrow? Where's your bride? Who will you bring to my royal banquet?

FOMA-TSAREVICH. No sweethearts in the swamp!

DANILA-TSAREVICH. No brides in the bog!

TSAR. Enough! The Tsar has spoken! Off you go, Ivan-Tsarevich. Follow your arrow and find its finder. As for me—I'm off to rule my Tsardom. If I don't keep inventing new laws, my empire will collapse before lunchtime!

Scene 2
The Swamp

(A swamp covered in mists. Mysterious greenish fires glow in the distance. IVAN-TSAREVICH makes his way through the quag with great difficulty.)

IVAN TSAREVICH. Well, this is a fine kettle of borscht! I've been squelching through this turgid swamp all day. Lost and alone in the gruesome gray woods. And now night's coming down like a bucketful of gravy. Lost and alone. What a skunky place! All the squashy ooze trying to suck me down, down into bubbling depths of the bog. *(He sits. Pours water out of one boot. Takes off the other boot, empties more water.)* Dark and getting darker. *(Pulling boots back on.)* I can't see the nose in front of my face. I'll never find that arrow. I'll head home and tell my father: "Dear Tsar, I'm very sorry to say, I don't think I can get married today." *(He is about to leave but swamp fires stand in his way. They dance around him, luring him on. Some of the fires go off and secretly bring back in a covered VASILISA as a frog.)* Out of my way, you swamp fire creatures. You flickery beasts of the slobbery quag—Where are you taking me? You're going to swallow me alive. No!

(Suddenly the swamp fires vanish. Stars appear in the sky. A new moon sails out. Its rays illuminate VASILISA in the form of a frog sitting in the swamp. On the frog's head is a shining crown. In her paws, she holds the gold arrow.)

VASILISA. Greetings, Ivan-Tsarevich.

IVAN-TSAREVICH. You speak human? And in a human voice?

VASILISA. There are many wonders in the world, more than you could ever imagine. Now we must talk together, Ivan-Tsarevich, for I am your bride-to-be.

IVAN-TSAREVICH. Just a moment, Frog Lady. I think you'd better hand back that arrow and hop off home. I'm the royal son of the royal Tsar. How could I marry you? Of course you're very attractive, and I'm very fond of green, of course, but you do remain, um, an amphibian. And Princes don't normally marry amphibians.

VASILISA. Are you scared of what people might say? Is that it, Ivan-Tsarevich? Are you scared they would laugh?

IVAN-TSAREVICH. *(To himself.)* I'm a royal muggins, a supper-galoot! I've dug my own muddy grave. But what can I do? I'm a good prince, I can't break my promise. Looks like I'll have to marry a frog.

VASILISA. Oh, Ivan-Tsarevich, would you really do that for the sake of your royal vow?

IVAN-TSAREVICH. Well, yes, I would. That's it. There's nothing more to say, is there? You'll be able to laugh and grow fat in the gardens of the Tsar. Quite a leap from your little hummock in the swamp, isn't it? I hope you're satisfied.

VASILISA. It's not the palace gardens that will make me happy.

IVAN-TSAREVICH. You shall have your own marble tub with running water. You'll be able to splash around and remember the days in the dear old swamp.

VASILISA. That's very kind. But I don't want to be any trouble.

IVAN-TSAREVICH. It's no trouble at all. And on Saturdays I'll stroll over to the slaughterhouse and collect you a sack full of flies. You could have a bluebottle banquet. *(Suddenly remembers the TSAR's planned banquet, puts his head in his hands.)* Oh, the banquet! I feel like a log just fell on my head. I forgot—tomorrow the Tsar's going to throw a great feast. He ordered each of his sons' brides to bake him a royal loaf of fancy bread and embroider him a glorious tablecloth with royal roosters. And they have to present these presents in person.

VASILISA. Why not?

IVAN-TSAREVICH. Think. Your loaf of bread would stink of the swamp. And your roosters would probably go croak-a-doodle-croak!

VASILISA. Don't you worry your handsome little head, Ivan-Tsarevich. I'll manage.

IVAN-TSAREVICH. Yes? All right, so you bake the loaf, you embroider the tablecloth. But how can I show you to my father? He'll throw a royal fit. Well, maybe you could fix a veil over your snout. I mean, I think you look great, but I've gotten used to you and my father, well he's kind of an old-fashioned Tsar—

VASILISA. Ivan-Tsarevich.

IVAN-TSAREVICH Yes?

VASILISA. Stop worrying.

IVAN-TSAREVICH. What else can I do?

VASILISA. Go home and go to bed. Everything'll look better in the morning.

IVAN-TSAREVICH. And the banquet?

VASILISA. Go to the banquet. Sit silently and bide your time. But as soon as you hear a rumbling and a rattling in the sky, just say this: "Here comes my frog!"

IVAN-TSAREVICH. "Here comes my frog!"?

VASILISA. That's right.

IVAN-TSAREVICH. Whatever you say. *(Yawns.)* I need some sleep. *(Starts to leave, then looks back.)* So, green, so deeply green, such a sweet shade of green—my little frog bride.

(IVAN-TSAREVICH leaves.)

VASILISA. Bride? Nevesta? That's the magical word, Ivan-Tsarevich. You called me your bride.

(Arrow music. Green flashes of light. Where the frog has been standing we now see VASILISA THE FAIR, dressed in gleaming and rich attire. In her hands she holds the empty green frog's skin.)

VASILISA. *(Claps her hands and calls.)*
Miller of the waving wheat
Come grind us finest flour to eat.
Bakers of the golden bread
There's a Tsar who must be fed.
Fly to me through the midnight air—
Come to Vasilisa the Fair!

(Ensemble dance—"The Making of the Bread.")

VASILISA.
Embroiderers of glowing cloth
More delicate than any moth,
Bring your silk and needles with you
For there is magic work to do.
Fly through the midnight air—
Come to Vasilisa the Fair!

(Ensemble dance—"The Making of the Tablecloth."
Music fades away. VASILISA is presented with the loaf wrapped in silk and a parcel containing the tablecloth.)

VASILISA. Thank you, spaisbo. *(She claps her hands. Her helpers disappear.)* Yes! He called me his bride! Nevesta!

Scene 3
The Tsar's Palace

(The TSAR, FOMA-TSAREVICH, DANILA-TSAREVICH, AKULINA, PAVA, IVAN-TSAREVICH and the ENSEMBLE MEMBERS enter dancing. MUSICIANS entertain the TSAR by playing on wooden spoons. TUMBLERS join them, jumping, turning somersaults, turning cartwheels, etc. With a wave of his hand, the TSAR sends the performers packing.)

TSAR. Enough of the cabaret—the Tsar is hungry. My royal belly's growling like a lion. All the other brides are here. Where's yours?

IVAN-TSAREVICH. I expect she's powdering her snout—I mean her nose.

TSAR. And what sort of lady are we waiting for, anyway? What's she like, your sweetheart of the swamplands?

IVAN-TSAREVICH. Well, her eyes are very large, prominent eyes, yes—

AKULINA. Is her hair dark and mysterious like mine?

PAVA. Or fair and luminous, like mine?

IVAN-TSAREVICH. As for hair, well, she doesn't really go in for hair.

TSAR. You mean—she's a bald bride?

IVAN-TSAREVICH. Well, baldish, you know. But she's very lively.

FOMA-TSAREVICH. Does she dance?

DANILA-TSAREVICH. Can she ride?

IVAN-TSAREVICH. She's more inclined to swimming. And jumping.

TSAR. Jumping? Who needs a jumping Princess? What's her complexion like?

AKULINA. Is her skin like milk?

PAVA. Or like a peach?

IVAN-TSAREVICH. No, it's more like grass.

TSAR. Like grass. *(Thinks with his brain.)* You mean, she's GREEN?

IVAN-TSAREVICH. Well, green-ish.

FOMA-TSAREVICH. Are her feet very little?

AKULINA. Is her voice soft or harsh?

IVAN-TSAREVICH. She has big webbed feet and a very sweet croak.

TSAR. Ivan-Tsarevich, are you trying to tell us there's something unusual about your bride.

IVAN-TSAREVICH. Not really, she's just rather more attractive than your average frog.

TSAR. A what? A whatter whatter?

IVAN-TSAREVICH. A frog, Father.

TSAR. You're going to marry a frog?

IVAN-TSAREVICH. Don't blame me. You told me to shoot the arrow.

TSAR. Did I tell you to aim it at the grobsuggling swamp? Listen to him. Always taking back. And always right. Well, I hope your frog knows what kind of boy she is marrying.

AKULINA. I hope she doesn't give us all warts.

FOMA-TSAREVICH. Slimy green skin—

IVAN-TSAREVICH. Now that's a common misunderstanding. Frogs aren't slimy at all.

DANILA-TSAREVICH. What will the neighbors say?

IVAN-TSAREVICH. Why should they worry? Sometimes you marry a beautiful girl and she turns out to be a hog. Or even a snake.

AKULINA. Just what are you insinuating, dear brother?

PAVA. Is that some kind of nasty joke?

TSAR. *(Stamping.)* What's going on here? The royal Tsar is dying of hunger. And he's being kept waiting by a reptile.

IVAN-TSAREVICH. An amphibian, Father.

TSAR. I'll pass a law outlawing all toads and newts and salamanders and axolotls and—

(Suddenly there's a rumbling, rattling sound in the air. GUARDS rush in to protect the TSAR. AKULINA, PAVA, FOMA-TSAREVICH and DANILA-TSAREVICH are frightened.)

IVAN-TSAREVICH. Here comes my frog!

ALL. *(Astonished.)* Here comes your frog?

(Doors open wide and VASILISA THE FAIR appears in the doorway, covered from head to toe in a fine, gleaming green cloak.)

IVAN-TSAREVICH. Yes, here's my little frog.

VASILISA. *(With a curtsey.)* Good health to you, dear Master, dear Tsar.

(TSAR circles VASILISA. He is very eager to look under her veil, but then jerks back his hand, afraid of seeing some kind of monster.)

TSAR. And good health to you. What is your name?

VASILISA. They call me Vasilisa.

IVAN-TSAREVICH. *(To himself.)* Vasilisa, I've heard that name. Vasilisa the Fair ….

TSAR. You may be a frog, Vasilisa, but there is something royal about you. You walk like a Princess.

FOMA-TSAREVICH. *(Mocking.)* A frog princess?

TSAR. Come, now, my three little brides, let's see how lovingly you have prepared your gifts for me. The loaves first, please.

(AKULINA comes forward proudly and hands the bread she has baked to the TSAR.)

AKULINA. Try one tiny bite, dear Tsar, and you'll never be able to put it down.

(TSAR tries to break a piece off the loaf, but it's very under-baked. The dough stretches and sticks to his hands and clothes.)

TSAR. Yuck! It's all under-done and sticky. *(Yells.)* Somebody get this schluckamucky dough off of me! *(AKULINA and FOMA-TSAREVICH try to help but only make matters far worse.)* You call that—putty—fit for a Tsar? *(To PAVA.)* Well now, daughter of the seller of silken suits—it's your turn. Pray present your loaf to your starving Tsar. *(PAVA brings in a plate. On it is a loaf of fancy bread burned so black it looks like charcoal.)* I've heard of black bread, but this—

PAVA. Just a tiny bit overdone on the outside. But it's so good and sweet, once you put it in your mouth you won't be able to spit it out.

(TSAR breaks off a piece, tries it. Starts coughing and choking. DANILA-TSAREVICH and PAVA rush to his aid, slapping his back.)

TSAR. Oy, oy, oy! That's enough. I don't dare look at what the frog cooked up for me. Soggy green bread I shouldn't wonder.

VASILISA. Oh please just look at it, dearest Tsar. You don't have to taste it.

(VASILISA hands the TSAR a dish. On it is a crusty light loaf of bread baked to look like a palace, with onion domes and battlements. All react in amazement.)

TSAR. Looks good. Do I dare? Yes, I do dare. *(TSAR breaks off a piece and tastes it.)* So fragrant. So light! It melts on the tongue. O such beautiful bread should only be eaten on the Tsar's own birthday.

VASILISA. I will bake bread like this every morning for your breakfast.

TSAR. Oh my dear Vasilisa Frog, you have found the soft spot of the mighty Tsar. This bread is—splendofabulissimus!

ALL. *(Tasting.)* Splendofabulissimus!

AKULINA. *(To PAVA.)* That stupid frog tricked us!

PAVA. Wait till I get my claws into her green skin.

TSAR. And now the Tsar would like to examine the tablecloths which you have so cunningly embroidered with strutting roosters.

AKULINA. *(Stepping forward.)* Dear Tsar and Father, look at mine!

TSAR. What's this. Three stitches, and all of the crooked? That's not cunning embroidery. It's an apology for a dishrag!

PAVA. Mine, mine, look at mine! I've been working really hard. I used up seven miles of Daddy's silk.

(TSAR takes PAVA's tablecloth and unfolds it. Threads of all colors stick out in all directions. He pricks his finger on a needle left in the embroidery. He sucks his wounded finger.)

TSAR. It's a ragmuffled wreck of a tablecloth, it's got no roosters on it and you left a needle in it that pricked my royal finger and there's blood! *(To VASILISA.)* That's enough tablecloths. I won't unfold it.

VASILISA. Good Master and Tsar, if you don't like it, give it to the beggars at your gates.

(The ENSEMBLE unfolds the tablecloth, displaying wonderful roosters. A loud series of cockcrows is heard.)

TSAR. It cock-a-doodle dooed! It's the most beautiful tablecloth in the world, dear Vasilisa.

AKULINA. *(To PAVA.)* She's done it again!

PAVA. She humiliated us!

AKULINA. She must be a monster. Look how she keeps herself all covered up.

PAVA. Let's tear off her cloak. Then everyone can see how disgusting she is.

(They rush at VASILISA from both sides and try to tear off her cloak.)

AKULINA. Take a good look, oh Tsar!

PAVA. See how ugly she is.

(AKULINA and PAVA tear the cloak from VASILISA. All are struck dumb by the beauty of VASILISA THE FAIR.)

TSAR. *(To IVAN-TSAREVICH.)* You clucknoddle! I thought you said she was a frog!

IVAN-TSAREVICH. It's a dream. Who are you?

VASILISA. Your bride, Vasilisa.

IVAN-TSAREVICH. Vasilisa the Fair!

TSAR. Come to me, my sons, all our worries are over. Let the celebration begin?

(A celebration dance takes place. Toward the end of it, VASILISA and IVAN-TSAREVICH move away to be alone.)

IVAN-TSAREVICH. You're so beautiful now. Prekraznaya. Of course. You make a very beautiful frog—but as a woman! What's wrong, my love?

VASILISA. There's something I have to find and fetch. Our happiness depends on it.

IVAN-TSAREVICH. I can't bear to let you out of my sight.

VASILISA. I'll be back in a moment. I must go alone.

IVAN-TSAREVICH. I must come with you.

VASILISA. You're so stubborn. Very well. Please go get my cloak.

IVAN-TSAREVICH. Good.

(IVAN-TSAREVICH goes to fetch Vasilisa's cloak, which the ENSEMBLE members have taken offstage.)

VASILISA. *(Whispers, gesturing.)*
Through the wild and whirling sky
To the swamplands let me fly!

(VASILISA vanishes. IVAN-TSAREVICH returns with Vasilisa's cloak, double-takes, finding her gone.)

IVAN-TSAREVICH. —Vasilisa! She vanished! *(A figure in a cloak appears beside him.)* Vasilisa! *(The figure turns. It is apparently an old beggar. In fact, the figure is KASHCHEY THE DEATHLESS, a wicked wizard who is the father of VASILISA.)* I thought you were her! You're a poor old beggar.

KASHCHEY. Just an old beggar, all skin and bone. I wander through this harsh world all alone.

IVAN-TSAREVICH. Can I help you? I'm the son of the Tsar.

KASHCHEY. Ivan-Tsarevich, I know who you are. And I've come to help *you,* for I bring you this day something shameful which was hidden away in the murk of the swamps where the lizards grin—a wedding present—your bride's frog skin!

(KASHCHEY produces the green skin from his cloak and holds it out.)

IVAN-TSAREVICH. What do I want with the skin of a frog?

KASHCHEY. This is the skin Vasilisa wore and she will become a frog once more and she will forget your face and your name—unless this skin burns in the flame. So take it, burn it.

IVAN-TSAREVICH. *(Taking the skin.)* Thank you, kind beggar. I'll save you, Vasilisa, you'll never be a frog again.

(KASHCHEY comes to the front of the stage and throws off his beggar's cloak, revealing himself as a wizard in shining silver clothes.)

KASHCHEY. *(To audience, laughing maliciously.)* And here I stand, and I laugh at the world. I am the greatest and wickedest wizard in all Russia. My name is Kashchey the Deathless, for I cannot die. Vasilisa the Fair is my daughter, but she will never be Ivan-Tsarevich's bride. For I have promised her to the Tsar of All the Seas and Oceans. Now I'll hide and see how well my trick works.

(KASHCHEY hides and watches. IVAN-TSAREVICH rushes to the stove with the frog skin.)

IVAN-TSAREVICH. You miserable raggedy green skin! I'll toss you in the stove and that's the end of you. *(He does so, puts more wood in the stove and blows on the fire.)*
Log of birchwood, flare and flame.
Long of pinewood, do the same.
Log of oak, go up in smoke.
Good, now it's beginning to roar. Burn to ashes, you horrible frog skin.

(Green flames shoot out of the stove, lighting up the chamber. Thunder booms. KASHCHEY laughs. VASILISA runs into the room.)

VASILISA. The frog skin! Too late. Ivan-Tsarevich—if only you'd waited or me to come back! I would have been yours forever.

IVAN-TSAREVICH. But you are mine.

VASILISA. I can't be. My father is Kashchey the Deathless, a powerful and wicked wizard. He promised me to the Tsar of All the Seas and Oceans. He's a great, blue giant with a beard down to his toes. I refused to marry him. So my father turned me into a frog for three years as a punishment. Those three years would have been up in just a few moments. But now I can't return the frog skin and that means—

KASHCHEY. *(Emerging from his hiding place.)* That means now I can take you home to the Kingdom of Never and to the blue arms of the Tsar of All the Seas and Oceans.

IVAN-TSAREVICH. You may be Vasilisa's father, but you're a villain. I'm going to turn you inside out.

VASILISA. Nobody can defeat him. He keeps his power and his death hidden in a golden needle.

IVAN-TSAREVICH. Where is the needle?

KASHCHEY. Hidden where nobody knows. *(Takes VASILISA's arm.)* Come with me now.

IVAN-TSAREVICH. I'll follow you to the Kingdom of Never.

VASILISA. It's far, very far, beyond the Thrice Ninth Land. Look! *(ENSEMBLE members bring in three iron walking sticks, three iron loaves and three pairs of iron boots.)* To reach the Kingdom of Never you must eat these three iron loaves and wear out these three iron walking sticks and three iron pairs of boots.

KASHCHEY. Come Vasilisa!

VASILISA. Ivan-Tsarevich!

(Thunder. Lights go out. Flashes. When lights come on, IVAN-TSAREVICH is alone.)

IVAN-TSAREVICH. Vasilisa!

(Exit IVAN-TSAREVICH, with all the iron implements in his arms as ENSEMBLE members enter with birch tree branches.)

Scene 4
The Forest

(A path through a forest and the lair of MISHA-MEDVED, the bear, created by the ENSEMBLE. Birdsong. Enter KASHCHEY THE

DEATHLESS. He wears a sword and drags VASILISA. Ahead of them three paths diverge.)

KASHCHEY. Hurry up! Hurry up! Down this path!

VASILISA. I'm not used to running. For the past two years and eleven moths I've had to hop. My legs have been working together all that time. *(Demonstrates hopping.)* They're not used to working one by one. *(Demonstrates awkward running.)* Let them have a rest.

(VASILISA sits down on a tree stump.)

KASHCHEY. Only for a minute. Then we must be on our way or we'll be late for your wedding. Kashchey the Deathless may have a few little faults—like wickedness—but he is never never late.

VASILISA. How can I marry this Tsar of All the Seas and Oceans? I've never even seen him.

KASHCHEY. But he's seen pictures of you.

VASILISA. As a woman or as a frog?

KASHCHEY. Both. And he was enchanted with both of you.

VASILISA. Well, I'm not enchanted by him.

KASHCHEY. You will be when you see him.

VASILISA. Is he tall?

KASHCHEY. Tall as a mountain.

VASILISA. Is he kind?

KASHCHEY. That depends on the weather.

VASILISA. Is he blue all over?

KASHCHEY. As far as I know. *(Angrily.)* Have you got anything against blue?

VASILISA. It's one of my favorite colors. But I'm promised to another.

KASHCHEY. Well you can forget another. He'll have too much of a bellyache from those iron loaves to follow you very far. And even if he does find our trail…. Excuse me a moment. I must just give my instructions to the creature who lives in this lair.

(KASHCHEY crawls into the lair of the fire-breathing bear.)

VASILISA. I'm sure my Prince isn't far away. I can feel it in my heart. But how can I show him which path to follow? *(Scratches her head.)* Ah, that's it.

(VASILISA removes a ribbon from her hair and hangs it on a branch beside the path which KASHCHEY indicated they are to follow. KASHCHEY emerges grumpily from the lair.)

KASHCHEY. Pah! Dust and spiders!
VASILISA. Who have you been talking to in that cave, Father?
KASHCHEY. A foolish, slovenly beast—but that's no concern of yours. Come! Your wedding feast awaits.

(KASHCHEY drags VASILISA down the path and away. The sound of sobbing is heard. Then, out of the lair crawls MISHA-MEDVED, THE FIRE-BREATHING BEAR. [Medved is Russian for bear.] MISHA is sad, sobbing to himself. He drags himself to the tree stump and sits down.)

MISHA. Boo-hoo-hoo. Boo-hoo-hoo. Boo-hoo-hoo-hoo-hooshki-boo! I'd love to be snuffling around the wild raspberry bushes, but I have to sit here like a bear on a tree-stump.

You know you can search the whole forest, search the whole of Russian, search the whole world and go through your pockets as well—you'll never find a glummer or a gloomier beast than yours truly, Misha the Bear. D'you know why? I'm droopy and downcast, in the dumps and the doldrums because I am a kind kind of bear. Kindness, that's my trouble. I feel sorry for everybody. I feel sorry for you. And sorrier for me. Can't help it, that' the way I was born. The moment I popped out of my mother I said sorry to her and sorry to my father and sorry to the midwife. Soft-hearted and sentimental. That's me. But that doesn't suit old Bonesy. That's what I call Kashchey the Deathless.

You know what he's done? He's ordered me to stay in this forest forever. Well, it's not a bad forest, if you like forests. But he's turned me into a fire-breathing bear. So I have to burn up every creature that passes by, whether they're flying, skipping, hopping, crawling or walking. I hate to do it, but I burn 'em up. Floosh!

That's why I'm so lonely. Whenever I see anybody in the distance I shout to warm them, hey get out of here, run for your life, save your skin or you'll be sizzled like a sausage. I've lost count of how many rabbits have gone up in flames. And foxes—they're so quick— there's no time to warm them—suddenly it's fried fox. *(Sobs.)* I can't bear it. Still, it looks like a quiet afternoon. I'll lie down and take a little nap.

(MISHA lies down, head in his paws, falls asleep. IVAN-TSAREVICH is heard in the distance.
Enter IVAN-TSAREVICH. He carries an iron walking stick and the last slice of iron bread. He sits down wearily.)

IVAN-TSAREVICH. I've walked and walked till I've worn out the three pairs of iron boots. I've eaten and eaten till I've chewed up two of the three iron loaves. Just one slice left of the last one. I'm going to finish it now. I've only lost five teeth so far. Wish me luck. Here goes. *(IVAN-TSAREVICH chews bravely. On tooth comes out.)* Ow! That was my favorite gnasher.

(IVAN-TSAREVICH inspects the tooth affectionately, pockets it, returns to chewing and finishes the slice.)

MISHA. *(Waking and jumping up.)* Hold it! Stop, stop right where you are, young man. One step further and I'll be obliged to burn you up.

IVAN-TSAREVICH. Burn me up? You should be ashamed.

MISHA. I am ashamed. All over. But I can't help it. I've been placed under a burn 'em up spell. Floosh! The flames jump out of my mouth. And I burn 'em up.

IVAN-TSAREVICH. But you seem like a kindly bear.

MISHA. You're so right.

IVAN-TSAREVICH. Well, couldn't you just keep your jaws clamped tight shut for ten ticks while I sprint by?

MISHA. That's a very good idea and I'd love to do it—but I can't. The spell won't let me. Take one more step and you'll be burned to a crisp or the ashes of a crisp. Floosh! Like that.

IVAN-TSAREVICH. Is there some way to free you from this burn 'em up spell?

MISHA. Oh yes. It's easy as pie. But totally impossible.

IVAN-TSAREVICH. What does that mean?

MISHA. All you have to do is blow in my right ear. Then the magic flame will fly out through my left ear. And all my burn 'em up powers will vanish.

IVAN-TSAREVICH. Let's try it.

MISHA. There's only one problem.

IVAN-TSAREVICH. Which is?

MISHA. You'd be burned to blazes before you could blow in my right ear. That's what Kashchey the Deathless has done to me. Boo-hoo. Boo-hoo-hooshki.

IVAN-TSAREVICH. No use crying. We've got to think with our brains.

MISHA. You're right. Let's think with our brains. *(Both think hard.)* No use.

IVAN-TSAREVICH. Think harder.

MISHA. I thunk so hard my brain's boiling over.

IVAN-TSAREVICH. Mine too. *(Takes off his fur hat, fans himself.)* I know! Come on, hat! Do me a favor.

(IVAN-TSAREVICH throws his hat at MISHA. Flame shoots out of MISHA's mouth. The hat burns up. IVAN-TSAREVICH rushes up to MISHA and blows in his right ear. Flame comes out of his left ear, then goes out. MISHA, not understanding what's happened, covers his muzzle with his paws and cries bitterly.)

MISHA. Boo-hooshki! I've done it again. I burned him up. Such a pleasant young man. And now he's nothing but cinders. I'll never forgive myself—and it's not even my fault. I'm the most miserablest bear in the world. Boo-hooshki. *(IVAN-TSAREVICH comes up to MISHA and embraces him. MISHA pushes him away.)* It's no good. You can't comfort me. You're all burned up. Oaow!! You're alive. So who got burned?

IVAN-TSAREVICH. No one at all. I freed you from the spell, Misha. Now you can live happily ever after. You'll never have to burn 'em up again. You can spend your days picking raspberries or hunting for honeycombs.

MISHA. That's not the sort of bear I am. You're my friend, and

I'll never leave your side.

IVAN-TSAREVICH. But you don't know who I am or where I'm going.

MISHA. Tell me.

IVAN-TSAREVICH. I'm Ivan-Tsarevich and I'm off to the Kingdom of Never to rescue my sweetheart Vasilisa from Kashchey the Deathless.

MISHA. How sweet is your sweetheart?

IVAN-TSAREVICH. Vasilisa is sweeter than the honeycomb.

MISHA. All right, I'll come and help you. Ho, wait! I'll just fetch my Useful Bag.

(MISHA fetches a small sack from his lair, puts it on his shoulder.)

IVAN-TSAREVICH. What's it useful for?

MISHA. Keeping things in. Odd things. *(Looks in.)* For instance—a dried sardine, a bottle of olive oil and an old bone.

IVAN-TSAREVICH. Useful?

MISHA. You never know. And it's a Useful Bag for when I find the Sugar Plum Tree.

IVAN-TSAREVICH. The Sugar Plum Tree?

MISHA. Right, Kashchey the Deathless told me it grows in the Land of Never and one day he'd let me climb it if I was a very good fire-breathing bear.

IVAN-TSAREVICH. Kashchey's a liar. There's no such thing as a Sugar Plum Tree.

MISHA. Of course there is.

IVAN-TSAREVICH. I've never seen one.

MISHA. Have you ever seen the back of your neck?

IVAN-TSAREVICH. No.

MISHA. Well, that proves it. Somewhere, somehow, there must be a Sugar Plum Tree

IVAN-TSAREVICH. No time to daydream. We've got to rescue Vasilisa.

MISHA. But which way did she go? There's three paths.

(The paths are created by the ENSEMBLE.)

IVAN-TSAREVICH. Three paths. Hold on. What's this? *(Takes*

the ribbon off the branch of the tree.) It's still warm. It's from Vasilisa's hair. She must have gone this way—straight towards the setting sun.

MISHA. To the rescue of Vasilisa!

IVAN-TSAREVICH. Yes, to my Vasilisa!

(IVAN-TSAREVICH and MISHA set off down the path.)

ACT II

Scene 1
Baba Yaga's Hut

(A desolate place, scorched and mountainous. The ENSEMBLE creates a fence around the hut, but it is a fence made of human bones, topped by human skulls. The gate has a human hand for a bolt, a mouth with sharp teeth for a lock.

The hut itself is tall, wooden and menacing. It stands on two enormous hen's feet and can move around. But when we first see it, the hut is squatting down so that we don't see the hen's feet. Beside the hut is an enormous stove with a large door. It is quite big enough to take two sheep at a time, or four children. A weeping willow tree, IVA, with a dangerous whippy branch, stands guard in front of the gate. Beyond the compound, seven roads lead away into the distance. It is evening and the sun is setting. The sky is bright orange.

Enter KASHCHEY THE DEATHLESS with VASILISA.)

VASILISA. Can't we stay and rest here?

KASHCHEY. There's no rest to be found in this place, daughter. This is the hut of my boney-legged sister, Baba Yaga, who eats nothing but people.

VASILISA. But if she's your sister, surely she'll spare us.

KASHCHEY. I am the Deathless One and even Baba Yaga couldn't kill me. But you are young and tender and she'd roast you in her terrible oven. Come, child, or we'll be late for your wedding.

VASILISA. Ivan-Tsarevich will stop this ridiculous marriage.

KASHCHEY. I'm sure he'll try. I can tell that he's following us with that treacherous bear. But Baba Yaga will take care of them.

VASILISA. Where is your sister now?

KASHCHEY. Let's find out! Sabaka! Koshka!

(STROGANOV-SABAKA, a fearsome dog, and GOLUBTSY-KOSHKA,

a terrifying cat, bound out from behind the hut, barking, snarling and spitting.)

KASHCHEY. Sabaka, sit! Koshka, be still!

(The cat and dog sit watchfully.)

KASHCHEY. Where is Baba Yaga tonight?

STROGANOV-SABAKA. She has gone out riding across the skies.

GOLUBTSY-KOSHKA. She has gone out hunting, hunting for children.

STROGANOV-SABAKA. But there are no children tonight in the forest.

GOLUBTSY-KOSHKA. So Baba Yaga will come home with a belly full of anger.

KASHCHEY. Good Sabaka, good Koshka, I must warn you. A Prince and a bear will come to this hut tonight. They are my enemies and the enemies of Baba Yaga.

STROGANOV-SABAKA. Then Baba Yaga's Iva tree will whip them.

(IVA demonstrates its whippiness.)

GOLUBTSY-KOSHKA. And Zamok, the gate, will scream a warning when they open it.

(ZAMOK the gate screams as KASHCHEY opens it.)

STROGANOV-SABAKA. And I will tear the Prince from top to toes.

GOLUBTSY-KOSHKA. And I'll scratch the bear till he's bald as the moon.

KASHCHEY. Good dog, good cat. *(KASHCHEY throws them each a crust, which they devour.)* Come Vasilisa, follow me.

(He takes one of the seven roads leading from the hut. STROGANOV-SABAKA and GOLUBTSY-KOSHKA retreat behind the hut again.

VASILISA waits.)

VASILISA. The way divides into so many paths. Ivan-Tsarevich may be clever enough to defeat Baba Yaga. But how will he know which one to take?

KASHCHEY. *(Off.)* Vasilisa!

VASILISA. I'll leave a brooch to show him the way. *(VASILISA takes a brooch from her dress and places it on the path.)* A very small brooch no one else will notice.

KASHCHEY. *(Off.)* Vasilisa. Your bridegroom awaits!

VASILISA. Coming, Father.

(Exit VASILISA. It's getting darker. Enter, cautiously, IVAN-TSAREVICH and MISHA.)

MISHA. That's the most disgustingest garden fence I've ever seen. Shaped like human bones and skulls—what bad taste.

IVAN-TSAREVICH. Those are real bones and skulls.

MISHA. They're real! Yaraagh! Maybe I've brought you the wrong way. I'm sorry.

IVAN-TSAREVICH. Look, will you stop apologizing Misha? There's nothing to be sorry about.

MISHA. Yes. You're right. I'm sorry.

IVAN-TSAREVICH. There you go again.

MISHA. So I do. It's a bad habit. Sorry.

IVAN-TSAREVICH. That's enough.

MISHA. Yes. Of course. I'm very—

IVAN-TSAREVICH. STOP IT!

MISHA. Pw! Hmmm. I won't say it again.

IVAN-TSAREVICH. You swear?

MISHA. I swear, with the deepest swear of a bear. Watch out for that tree!

(IVAN-TSAREVICH and MISHA duck as IVA the tree whips at them.)

IVAN-TSAREVICH. Come on, through this gate!

(IVAN-TSAREVICH unbolts and unlocks ZAMOK the gate, but as he swings it open it screams aloud.)

ZAMOK. Baba Yaga! Baba Yaga!

(IVAN-TSAREVICH shuts ZAMOK, which stops the screaming. But out leap STROGANOV-SABAKA and GOLUBTSY-KOSHKA, snarling and spitting.)

STROGANOV-SABAKA. Here comes the Tsarevich!

GOLUBTSY-KOSHKA. Here comes Misha!

STROGANOV-SABAKA. My teeth will tear you from top to toe.

GOLUBTSY-KOSHKA. I'll scratch you till you're bald as the moon.

MISHA. That's no way to welcome strangers.

(STROGANOV-SABAKA and GOLUBTSY-KOSHKA advance.)

IVAN-TSAREVICH. Back into the hut, then slam the door on them.

MISHA. I'm with you, Ivan-Tsarevich. *(IVAN-TSAREVICH and MISHA back towards the hut, but the hut rises on it's two chicken feet and backs away. After a couple of tries, IVAN-TSAREVICH and MISHA realize what's happening.)* A hut on chicken's feet!

IVAN-TSAREVICH. Run for your life!

(They move, but the hut chases them and they are face to face with STROGANOV-SABAKA and GOLUBTSY-KOSHKA again. Round the fence comes Baba Yaga. She is a terrible witch and, as in all the Baba Yaga stories, rides in a mortar with a pestle by her side, sweeping away her tracks with a great broom.)

STROGANOV-SABAKA and GOLUBTSY-KOSHKA. Baba Yaga! Baba Yaga!

BABA YAGA. Meat and bones! Russian meat and Russian bones! What brave creatures seek to be the guests of bone-gobbling Baba Yaga? Stand back, Iva. *(IVA the tree holds back its branch.)* Open gate Zamok! *(ZAMOK the gate opens for her, closes behind her.)* Lie down, Sabaka! Down, Koshka! *(They obey.)* Make room for me, Chicken Feet. *(The hut moves back politely. BABA YAGA con-*

fronts IVAN-TSAREVICH and MISHA.) What are your names? Come on, don't be shy. How can I eat you if we've not been introduced? I am Baba Yaga, the boney-legged sister of Kashchey the Deathless.

IVAN-TSAREVICH. I am Ivan-Tsarevich, son of the Tsar of all the Russians, betrothed to Vasilisa the Fair.

BABA YAGA. The frog woman? Croak, croak, what a joke!

IVAN-TSAREVICH. She once was a frog, but when she was, she was one million times as beautiful as you, Baba Yaga.

BABA YAGA. I don't try to be beautiful. All I want is meat and bones. And who are you?

MISHA. I am Misha, the fire-breathing bear.

BABA YAGA. Then you can light my stove, for I love roast medved.

MISHA. I'm very sorry—

IVAN-TSAREVICH. Misha!

MISHA. I forgot. Um. My fire seems to have gone out.

BABA YAGA. Sit down both of you and don't try to escape. All roads end at my house.

IVAN-TSAREVICH. Why is that?

BABA YAGA. Because I'm going to chew your flesh and munch your bones, that's why.

MISHA. We could go pick you some mushrooms—

BABA YAGA. Don't try to play tricks on Baba Yaga!

MISHA. Right. I'm sorry. Oh.

IVAN-TSAREVICH. All right, Misha. Baba Yaga, I hate to say so, but I think you've made a mistake.

BABA YAGA. And I think you'll make a nice steak—ha ha!

IVAN-TSAREVICH. I don't think I will. Have you ever eaten the son of a Tsar? I'm sure you're more used to mice and cockroaches.

BABA YAGA. What's so special about Tsar's sons. I've eaten hundreds of *people*, all kinds of people. Easy. First you simply scare them silly.

MISH. You're doing very well.

BABA YAGA. —Really frighten them. Fear makes them lovely and tender, you see. When people are scared they get all soft, chewy as baby rabbits. Then I grinds them up and I gulps them down.

MISHA. I can I imagine.

IVAN-TSAREVICH. But first you've got to terrify us? Come on, we don't scare so easily.

MISHA. Don't we?

BABA YAGA. *(Chants.)*
Demons of the air fly down
Spreading terror all around.
Fiery goblins of the night
Dance and howl and pinch and bite ...

(All the skulls on the fence light up with fire. All kinds of evil SPIRITS emerge—swamp spirits covered with moss, forest spirits with big noses and ears, wood goblins with arms dangling to the ground, bats, river mermaids and other ghosts of the woods. They all whirl in a mad dance around IVAN-TSAREVICH and MISHA.)

SPIRITS. *(Howling and yelling.)* Come to us! Come to us. Squeeze 'em. Tickle 'em. Tease 'em. Tear 'em.

(At the end of the dance, IVAN-TSAREVICH and MISHA fall, exhausted.)

BABA YAGA. *(Triumphant.)* Good! Now I can have my dinner. Let me feel your arm, Tsarevich. It should be as soft as oatmeal by now. *(Hiding his iron walking stick in his sleeve, IVAN-TSAREVICH extends it to BABA YAGA.)* It's hard as iron. Nobody could chew that. You're a solid stone pig! Nothing scares you. Off you go, you no-good demons. *(SPIRITS vanish.)* Ah, but don't think you're going to escape from me. I'll have my Chicken Feet hut trample you both into pulp. Come here, Chicken Feet!

(The hut approaches.)

MISHA. I'm quite an old medved, you know, older than I look. Quite a lot of fat and gristle.

BABA YAGA. Fat and gristle are two of my favorite things.

IVAN-TSAREVICH. Listen, Baba Yaga, trampling could make us tougher. Then you'd starve to death. What a shame that'd be!

BABA YAGA. *(Touched.)* It would, it would. I'd be deeply

sorry.

MISHA. And so would I.

BABA YAGA. What can we do about it?

IVAN-TSAREVICH. You could cook us.

MISHA. Shhh!

BABA YAGA. So I could.

MISHA. Starving's not so bad, you know.

BABA YAGA. A good slow roasting. Yes, that'd make you tender.

IVAN-TSAREVICH. It's worth trying.

MISHA. Yes, it's worth—it's a terrible idea! What sort of a friend are you?

IVAN-TSAREVICH. She's going to eat us sooner or later. Why make a fuss.

(BABA YAGA opens the oven door and slides out a long tray.)

BABA YAGA. All right, up you hop onto Baba Yaga's roasting tray. *(IVAN-TSAREVICH climbs onto the tray.)* You too, old medved. *(STROGANOV-SABAKA and GOLUBTSY-KOSHKA threaten MISHA, who climbs on too.)* Very good. No, not that way.

(IVAN-TSAREVICH has his legs up so the tray won't fit back into the oven.)

IVAN-TSAREVICH. Like this?

(IVAN-TSAREVICH turns over, but now his arms are sticking out at the side.)

BABA YAGA. No. Arms in. *(IVAN-TSAREVICH and MISHA both assume difficult positions. Furious.)* Not that way! Not that way!

IVAN-TSAREVICH. *(Sighing.)* We'll never get it right.

MISHA. *(Who has caught on by now.)* I'm afraid you'll have to show us.

(Deathly pause. Has BABA YAGA seen through their trick? Er, no.)

BABA YAGA. It's easy, you nincompoops! Get off my roasting

tray!

(IVAN-TSAREVICH and MISHA jump off the tray. BABA YAGA climbs on and lies down neatly.)

IVAN-TSAREVICH Oh, *now* I see.
MISHA. Looks comfortable.
BABA YAGA. Oh, it is.
IVAN-TSAREVICH. Here we go then!

(IVAN-TSAREVICH and MISHA slide the tray into the oven and slam the doors on BABA-YAGA. Her yells of rage stop when the oven doors close.)

STROGANOV-SABAKA. It's not quite as easy as that, Ivan-Tsarevich.
GOLUBTSY-KOSHKA. Because now we're going to tear you to pieces.

(STROGANOV-SABAKA and GOLUBTSY-KOSHKA advance.)

MISHA. Lucky I remembered my Useful Bag. *(Reaches into the bag. To STROGANOV-SABAKA.)* An old bone for you, my friend. *(To GOLUBTSY-KOSHKA.)* And a dried sardine for you. *(They devour them.)* Come on, Ivan-Tsarevich.
IVAN-TSAREVICH. But Zamok the gate will scream and deafen us.
MISHA. *(Reaching into his bag.)* Not if I oil its bony hinges with my olive oil. *(As IVA the tree draws back its whipping branch.)* Um, I forgot the Iva tree would whip us to death.
IVAN-TSAREVICH. Don't say that word! I kept the ribbon Vasilisa left for me.

(IVAN-TSAREVICH ties back IVA the tree's branch with the ribbon and MISHA oils ZAMOK the gate.)

ZAMOK. *(As they open it.)* Spasiba. Thank you, Misha.
MISHA. Pazhalsta.

IVA. Spasiba. Thank you, Ivan-Tsarevich, for the beautiful ribbon. Farewell.

IVAN-TSAREVICH. Dasvedanya.

MISHA. Excuse me, talking tree. Do you know where a bear might find the Sugar Plum Tree?

IVA. The Sugar Plum Tree?

MISHA. Yes?

IVA. Never heard of it.

MISHA. So it goes. Ah well, I'll take this skull as a souvenir.

(MISHA pops the skull from the fence into his Useful Bag.)

IVAN-TSAREVICH. So many paths! Which way should we go?

MISHA. Look! Something's shining on this path.

IVAN-TSAREVICH. *(Picking it up.)* It's a tiny brooch. *(Examines it.)* A brooch from Vasilisa's dress. This must be the right path. *(IVAN-TSAREVICH taps and waves his iron walking stick—it crumbles to nothing in his hand.)* Look! The third walking stick! It's crumbled to dust. That means we've nearly reached the Kingdom of Never. Hurry Misha, before we're too late.

(Exit IVAN-TSAREVICH and MISHA down the path. An angry BABA YAGA bursts out of the oven, hair badly singed, face and hands smeared with soot.)

BABA YAGA. They tricked me! And what did my servants do? Did you tear them to pieces or scratch them to bits?

STROGANOV-SABAKA and GOLUBTSY-KOSHKA. No we didn't, Baba Yaga.

BABA YAGA. Did you deafen them with screaming and whip them to death?

ZAMOK and IVA. No we didn't, Baba Yaga.

STROGANOV-SABAKA. He was kind to us, Baba Yaga. And you never were.

BABA YAGA. Fools! Traitors! You let my dinner escape!

(BABA YAGA takes up her broom and in a mad dance of rage, jumping up and down, attacks the dog, the cat, the gate and the tree. Comic/

ferocious music as the hut scuttles about, clucking like a hen.)

Scene 2
The Palace of Kashchey the Deathless

(As the scene opens, there is a dance. As it ends, SASHA-SHPIONKA, a spy for KASHCHEY, spots VASILISA.)

SASHA-SHPIONKA. *(Calling down stairs.)* Master! Master! Vasilisa's at the telescope again!

(SASHA-SHPIONKA exits as VASILISA enters, looks around, takes the telescope and stares through it, not at stars above, but at the road below.)

VASILISA. Ivan-Tsarevich, where are you? Did you find my ribbon and my brooch? Did Baba Yaga eat you up, bones and all? Or did you turn back because I'd once been a frog?

(KASHCHEY enters with SASHA-SHPIONKA.)

KASHCHEY. What are you doing, daughter?
VASILISA. Watching the stars and planets at their dancing.
SASHA-SHPIONKA. You won't see many stars at this time in the afternoon.
KASHCHEY. Why's the telescope pointed downwards?
SASHA-SHPIONKA. She's watching the road for Ivan-Tsarevich.
VASILISA. You, Sasha! You sneaky eavesdropping,. blabber-mouthed shpionka.
SASHA-SHPIONKA. I am personal assistant to Kashchey the Deathless. I am simply doing my job.
VASILISA. Personal assistant! Personal creeper and crawler!
KASHCHEY. I won't have my staff insulted. What a daughter! Even three years in a frog skin haven't taught you any manners. *(Stamps.)* You'll do as you're told and marry the Tsar of All the Seas

and Oceans.

VASILISA. No, dear Father. I know who I want to marry.

KASHCHEY. You're a fool and a dreamer, girl. Look at the wedding gifts the Tsar of the Oceans has sent you. *(KASHCHEY claps his hands. Hall lights up. ENSEMBLE members come on with treasure trunks of jewels. To VASILISA.)* This treasure is just a sample of the uncountable riches of your bridegroom. Great cliffs of coral. Hills of pearls. The lost treasure chests of a thousand sunken galleons—rubies, diamonds, emeralds and enough bars of gold to build a mountain.

VASILISA. Gold and jewels mean nothing to me. I love Ivan-Tsarevich.

(Aqua blue mist rises from the middle of the platform. The room is totally blue and it undulates. KASHCHEY, dragging VASILISA behind him, rushes to meet the SEA TSAR.)

KASHCHEY. Greetings, O Tsar of All the Seas and Oceans. Behold my daughter and your bride—Vasilisa the Fair!

SEA TSAR. *(In an enormous, deep, echoing voice.)* Greetings, Kashchey the Deathless! And my deepest greetings to you, Vasilisa Prekraznaya!

VASILISA. Greetings, O mighty Tsar.

KASHCHEY. Let us leave the happy couple to bill and coo.

(Exit KASHCHEY and SASHA-SHPIONKA. The SEA TSAR is with VASILISA. Both are shy. SASHA-SHPIONKA watches the road through the telescope.)

SEA TSAR. Vasilisa.

VASILISA. Yes.

SEA TSAR. You are very beautiful.

VASILISA. So they say. You are very—blue. Bluer than I thought.

SEA TSAR. Does blue repel you?

VASILISA. No, it's one of my favorite colors.

SEA TSAR. I suppose it won't be easy at first, living underwater, after breathing air for so long—

VASILISA. Well, I've spent nearly three years as a frog, so that's not really the problem—

SEA TSAR. Problem?

VASILISA. You see, I'm going to marry a Tsarevich—

SEA TSAR. A dry land Tsarevich?

VASILISA. Yes, Ivan-Tsarevich of Russia.

SEA TSAR. I know the lad. Not a bad swimmer. You're marrying him? Then you can't marry me.

VASILISA. I'm sorry. You are beautifully blue.

SEA TSAR. That's all right. I owed a debt to Kashchey and he told me I could only repay it by marrying you. But really, deep in my blue heart, I wanted to marry a mermaid.

VASILISA. May all your days together be happy as a school of dolphins.

SEA TSAR. *(Moved.)* Thank you. Spasiba. Vasilisa, to protect you, I give you this spell. If ever you are in mortal danger, call to me with these words: Moryea, Syuda, Syuda. Let the oceans roll!

VASILISA. Moryea, Syuda, Syuda, let the oceans roll. And what will happen if I use those words?

SEA TSAR. Your enemies will be crushed.

(KASHCHEY enters the hall.)

KASHCHEY. So, have the lovers planned their honeymoon?

SEA TSAR. There will be no honeymoon, there will be no wedding.

KASHCHEY. No wedding? Remember that old debt.

SEA TSAR. You told me Vasilisa longed to marry me. That was a lie, Kashchey the Deathless. The dept is canceled. Farewell, Vasilisa. In happy times and dangerous times I will always be your friend. Dasvedanya.

(Exit SEA TSAR.)

VASILISA. So now I'm free to marry my Tsarevich.

KASHCHEY. You'll never to free! Go to your room frogspawn!

(VASILISA exits. KASHCHEY paces, SASHA-SHPIONKA adjusts the

telescope.)

KASHCHEY. *(To himself.)* Who'd have a daughter? She drives me crazy! Never mind—if I can't bend her, I'll break her.

SASHA-SHPIONKA. *(Coming downstairs.)* Master, master, bad news. Ivan-Tsarevich is on his way to your palace with Misha the fire-breathing bear.

KASHCHEY. Impossible! If that bear didn't burn him, Baba Yaga would've gobbled him down, bones and all.

SASHA-SHPIONKA. But they didn't. I saw him through my own glass. He had all his bones. And a bear was strolling beside him.

KASHCHEY. For the first time in my life I feel an odd, chilly feeling. I think it must be what mortals call—fear. I'll need all my wisdom and cunning now.

SASHA-SHPIONKA. Think long, think hard, Kashchey, dear master. Who is wiser or cunninger than you?

KASHCHEY. Thoughts are easy. Ideas are hard. I know! Sasha-Shpionka, you shall serve me a little service. And as a reward, I shall bury you alive in precious jewels.

SASHA-SHPIONKA. That sounds good. What do I have to do?

KASHCHEY. I'll change your appearance, my lowly servant, change you so you look exactly like my daughter, Vasilisa the Fair. When Ivan-Tsarevich arrives, he will think you are his beloved.

SASHA-SHPIONKA. And then what? I can't simply stand there looking gorgeous. I'll have to talk to the Prince. I won't know what to say.

KASHCHEY. Listen. All you have to say is this: "Hurry, my love, the apple of my eye, to the stables of Kashchey the Deathless. Two raven-black steeds stand saddled there, waiting for us." Then you'll gallop away on the raven-black horses and they'll carry you to the river of fire. Ivan-Tsarevich's horse will be under a spell. It'll throw him in the fiery water.

SASHA-SHPIONKA. Serves him right. But what about me?

KASHCHEY. You'll turn around and gallop back here for your reward: a chest crammed with gems and jewels brighter than the stars at midnight.

SASHA-SHPIONKA. Gems and jewels? A chestful? Oh, my dearest master!

KASHCHEY. Not so fast!

SASHA-SHPIONKA. What?

KASHCHEY. Your voice. Repeat after me: "Health and happiness to you, Prince Ivan."

SASHA-SHPIONKA. Health and happiness to you, Prince Ivan.

KASHCHEY. Softer, you have to speak softer. Your voice should sound like a guitar with silver strings.

SASHA-SHPIONKA. Health and happiness to you, Prince Ivan.

KASHCHEY. Better. Much better. But remember, if the Prince suspects you're not Vasilisa, everything is ruined.

SASHA-SHPIONKA. *(Curtseying.)* Don't worry, Master. There'll be no mistakes. It might help if you gave me the treasure chest now, before you change me. Then I wouldn't tremble so much.

KASHCHEY. Afraid I won't pay you? Here, take it, you greedy ….

(KASHCHEY takes an iron-bound chest from the table and hands it to SASHA-SHPIONKA. She opens it. Rainbow flashes of light come from the open chest, the sparkling of multicolored jewels.)

SASHA-SHPIONKA. Rubies, gold and silver bars, diamonds like a thousand stars—I'm rich! Rich! It's all mine.

KASHCHEY. Careful, greed comes before a fall. *(During this exchange, VASILISA has crept up to the observatory and is looking through the telescope. KASHCHEY looks up and sees her. During the following, he performs a magic dance to help coax forth the spells.)* Now I must put my daughter into a trance. *(Chants, casting a spell over VASILISA.)*

Moaning and sighing,
Dreaming and crying,
Watery deep
Take my daughter to sleep,

(VASILISA sinks into the observatory chair.)

VASILISA. What's wrong? I'm sleepy, so sleepy. Like heavy black ravens spreading their wings over my eyes. Prince Ivan ….

(VASILISA falls into a magical sleep. Lights dim in the observatory.)

KASHCHEY. *(Casting a spell over SASHA-SHPIONKA.)*
Evil winds and breezes blow
Wicked streams and rivers flow
Change this wretch until she looks
like the Princess in storybooks.

(A peal of thunder. Rays of magical light. Another peal of thunder. Light returns. SASHA-SHPIONKA has been turned into VASI-LISA. She holds the treasure chest in her hands.
Shouts, clanging, weapons clanking outside. A GUARD runs in.)

GUARD. Danger, my lord! Ivan-Tsarevich and his bear have stormed over the gate. Any minute they'll be in the palace. Shall we roll out the cannons?

KASHCHEY. *(Calmly.)* No. This is my command. Throw wide the palace gates. Open all the doors. Let them walk in freely. *(The GUARD is dumbfounded. KASHCHEY dismisses him with a wave of his hand. GUARD runs out.)* Now it all depends on you, Sasha-Shpionka.

(KASHCHEY leaves hurriedly. IVAN-TSAREVICH runs into the hall, sword in hand. MISHA hobbles after him.)

IVAN-TSAREVICH. Vasilisa! Where are you?

SASHA-SHPIONKA. *(Stepping forward and speaking in a sugary voice.)* Health and happiness to you, Prince Ivan.

IVAN-TSAREVICH. *(Rushing to her.)* Vasilisa, my love, my life!

MISHA. *(Looking around.)* Oy, what a treasure!

SASHA-SHPIONKA. Hurry, my love, the apple of my eye, to the stables of Kashchey the Deathless. Two raven-black steeds stand saddled there, waiting for us.

IVAN-TSAREVICH. You better leave that chest here, my darling. It'd slow us up and we've got to escape.

SASHA-SHPIONKA. And leave these jewels behind?

IVAN-TSAREVICH. Why should we need jewels? Our love is far more precious.

(SASHA-SHPIONKA laughs nervously.)

MISHA. Don't dirty your little hands with that box. It's heavy. I, Misha, will carry it.

SASHA-SHPIONKA. No.

MISHA. Please. Pazhalstah.

(MISHA pulls at the treasure chest, but SASHA-SHPIONKA won't let go. Eager to help, MISHA pulls harder. Chest falls, SASHA-SHPIONKA, very angry, kicks MISHA so hard he flies head over heels. SASHA-SHPIONKA rushes to the chest.)

SASHA-SHPIONKA. You fzzy-brained buffoon! I'll have you turned into a rug. You nearly smashed my lovely treasure chest!

MISHA. This is your sweet Vasilisa?

IVAN-TSAREVICH. *(Shaken.)* Vasilisa would never speak to a bear like that. It's a trick! You're not Vasilisa! Witchcraft!

SASHA-SHPIONKA. *(Shouts.)* Kashchey! Master! Come here!

MISHA. No hurry! Last person we need right now is Kashchey the Deathless.

(A peal of thunder. Flashes of light and darkness. Lights come up and SASHA-SHPIONKA as herself is standing over the chest.
Lights up in observatory. VASILISA, roused from her trance, runs to IVAN-TSAREVICH.)

VASILISA. Ivan, my love!

IVAN-TSAREVICH. My Vasilisa! The real Vasilisa. I can tell by the kindness in your eyes. I know you.

VASILISA. Of course you do.

IVAN-TSAREVICH. But they've been playing tricks on me. *(Points at SASHA-SHPIONKA.)* She disguised herself as you. At first she had me fooled but—Misha! Hide her behind a pillar and make sure she's quiet as a mouse.

(MISHA puts his paw over SASHA-SHPIONKA's mouth and holds her tight.)

VASILISA. You should have stayed away. My father will kill both of us.

IVAN-TSAREVICH. I'll fight him.

VASILISA. Nobody can conquer him. His power and his death are contained in the tip of a golden needle.

IVAN-TSAREVICH. Where's it kept?

VASILISA. Hidden away where nobody knows. Wait. I know. My father made her look like me? Let's turn his own trick against him. I'll try to uncover my father's secret. Ivan-Tsarevich, you must hide, and hide that treasure, too. *(MISHA hides with SASHA-SHPIONKA. IVAN-TSAREVICH hides behind another column.)* Master! Dear Master! Danger!

(KASHCHEY comes running in.)

KASHCHEY. Sasha, where's Ivan-Tsarevich?

VASILISA. *(In SASHA-SHPIONKA's voice.)* Gone to the stables to tighten the horses' saddles. We're about to ride away. But I'm scared.

KASHCHEY. What's wrong?

VASILISA. I was talking with that Sea Tsar. And he said your secret golden needle has vanished away, that it's hiding place is empty. Your power over death has gone!

KASHCHEY. *(In terror.)* Impossible! Impossible! Open up, O secret place. Split open, rocks! Magic golden needle—appear!

(Rock walls move apart noisily and we see a long, shining golden needle.)

VASILISA. IVAN-TSAREVICH!!

(IVAN-TSAREVICH rushes in and is about to seize the needle.)

KASHCHEY. Let darkness fall!

IVAN-TSAREVICH. Where is it?

MISHA. Hold everything! Where's my Useful Bag? Right!

(MISHA produces the skull from his Useful Bag. It throws beams of light on the needle. IVAN-TSAREVICH grabs the needle and holds it aloft. VASILISA goes to his side. SASHA-SHPIONKA

joins KASHCHEY. Confrontation.)

IVAN-TSAREVICH. So we meet at last, Kashchey the Death-less. And now I am the master of the golden needle.
KASHCHEY. Are you a man?
IVAN-TSAREVICH. Of course.
KASHCHEY. Then fight me like a man.

(KASHCHEY draws his sword. IVAN-TSAREVICH passes the needle to MISHA and draws his sword. Sword fight. To and fro. Finally, SASHA-SHPIONKA trips IVAN-TSAREVICH, KASHCHEY stands over him.)

VASILISA. Moryea, Syuda, Syuda! Let the oceans roll!
KASHCHEY. In the heart, I think.

(KASHCHEY raises his sword.
Ocean music. SEA TSAR rises from the fountain.)

SEA TSAR.
Now I create a storm upon the land—
Seasickness strikes on very hand!
(All begin to sway, especially KASHCHEY. All are overcome with seasickness.) Pass Ivan-Tsarevich the golden needle, my brave bear.
MISHA. *(Reeling.)* Here, take it.

(MISHA passes the needle to IVAN-TSAREVICH, who raises it above his head.)

KASHCHEY. I curse you, every one of you, especially you, my daughter.
SEA TSAR. *(To IVAN-TSAREVICH.)* Behold! You end his power and bring his death.
MISHA. Floosh to you, Old Bonesy!

(IVAN-TSAREVICH breaks the golden needle. KASHCHEY cries out and falls with SASHA-SHPIONKA. ENSEMBLE members carry them out.)

IVAN-TSAREVICH. It's like waking up from a terrible dream—my own Vasilisa!

VASILISA. Ivan my love, you must be the bravest prince in all Russia.

IVAN-TSAREVICH. I'm the happiest man in the world.

VASILISA. And I'm the happiest woman.

MISHA. *(Butting in.)* And I'm the happiest bear. Happy, but hungry.

(Suddenly KASHCHEY's palace vanishes ...)

Scene 3
The Tsar's Palace

(... and we are in the Tsar of Russia's palace with the TSAR, DANILA-TSAREVICH, FOMA-TSAREVICH, PAVA and AKU-LINA. Beside them stands a shining and amazing tree. IVAN-TSAREVICH, VASILISA and MISHA join them.)

TSAR. Jubiloosination! Is it really you, Ivan-Tsarevich, my marvelously disobedient son? And you, most ollistracious Vasilisa? My son, you have brought joy to my heart. But what's this shaggedy growl-bag at my side?

IVAN-TSAREVICH. He's Misha, a brave and kindly bear who helped us on our way.

MISHA. Excuse me, Mr. Tsar, what kind of tree is that?

TSAR. An extremely rare specimen of the Sugar Plum Tree. Let me present it to you, gallant bear.

MISHA. The Sugar Plum Tree? For me? *(Thinks.)* Boo-hoo-hooshki!!

IVAN-TSAREVICH. Come on Foma-Tsarevich and Danila-Tsarevich, it's time to celebrate.

TSAR. I'll celebrate with a new law.

VASILISA. What's the new law, my new father?

TSAR. The Tsar of all Russians decrees that there shall be happy endings to the stories of all good men and women— *(MISHA taps him on the shoulder.)* —and bears!

(Music resumes. All dance or play instruments or both.)

THE END

PROPS

The Tsar's Palace
Stage Right
Golden arrows
Stage Left
Scroll
Seal
Bow
Golden arrow
Muffin

The Swamp
Stage Right
Golden arrow
10 embroidery needles
Vasilisa's bread under drape
Vasilisa's tablecloth

The Tsar's Palace
Stage Right
Sticky bread
Three-stitch tablecloth
Ragamuffin tablecloth
Small stove
3 iron loaves
3 iron walking sticks
3 pairs of iron boots
Stage Left
Burnt bread
Frog skin for stove

The Forest
Stage Right
Pair of birch tree branches
Stage Left
Tree stump
Useful Bag
Dried Sardine
Old bone
Bottle of olive oil
3 pair birch tree branches
Crumbling walking stick

Baba Yaga's Hut
Stage Right
Large oven
Yagamobile
Skull on a stick
Stage Left
Moon

Kashchey's Palace
Stage Right
Vasilisa's telescope
2 black telescopes
Sword with straight blade
Stage Left
Sasha's telescope
2 black telescopes
Treasure chests
Sword with curved blade

The Tsar's Palace
Stage Right
Maypole
Stage Left
Maypole
Sugar Plum Tree

PLAYS FOR CHILDREN
Blanche Marvin

Written in different styles ranging from Restoration comedy to Japanese Noh, this is a rich and varied two-volume collection of wonderful plays for children of all ages. They are ideal for school and professional productions. Audience participation is encouraged in each unique version of a fairy tale or holiday story.

Volume I

Birthday of the Infanta
The Firebird
The Legend of Scarface and Bluewater
The Pied Piper

Volume II

The Emperor's New Clothes
Sleeping Beauty
Cinderella
The Littlest Tailor
Arabian Nights
Peter and the Wolf
Alice in Wonderland
Pinocchio
The Red Dragon
Mr. Easter Bunny
Crowning Glory

9780573629518
VASILISA THE FAIR.

ISBN 0 573 62951 X   #23997